# VOLUME 7

# Jesus Raises Jairus' Daughter to the Burial of Jesus

# WORLD'S BIBLE STORY LIBRARY

## VOLUME 7

## Jesus Raises Jairus' Daughter to the Burial of Jesus

BY
### J. HAROLD GWYNNE, D.D.
ILLUSTRATED BY
### STEELE SAVAGE

The World Publishing Company
New York

# WORLD'S BIBLE STORY LIBRARY

is published by The World Publishing Company

Printed in the United States of America.

**WORLD PUBLISHING**
**TIMES MIRROR**

# Contents

## VOLUME 7

# Jesus Raises the Daughter of Jairus

*Matthew 9:18–30; Mark 5:21–43; Luke 8:40–56*

AFTER healing the man possessed with a legion of demons in the country of the Gadarenes, Jesus got in a boat with His disciples and crossed to the western shore of the Sea of Galilee at Capernaum. As soon as the boat touched the shore, a great crowd of people gathered around Jesus, for they were all waiting for Him. They wanted to hear more of His teachings, and to see more of His miracles of healing.

a large number

At once there ran forth from the crowd a man by the name of Jairus, a ruler of the synagogue, with a look of anxiety and distress on his face. He fell down at Jesus' feet and poured out his urgent plea: "My only little daughter is lying at the point of death. Come, Master, and lay your hands on her, so that she may be healed, and live." Jesus had compassion on this troubled father and started at once to go with him to his home.

But an interruption occurred. The crowd of people followed Jesus and thronged about a great crowd

a piece of clothing

Him. In this throng was a poor woman who had suffered from a dreadful disease for twelve long years. She had been to many physicians, but none of them had cured her. She had spent all her money, and her sickness had become worse instead of better. She had heard about Jesus' power to heal the sick, and she believed that He would be able to heal her. She thought she need only touch His garment to be cured. So she worked her way through the crowd and came up behind Jesus, and with timid and trembling fingers touched the fringe of His garment. And immediately the flow of blood that had wasted her body ceased; and she felt in her body that she was cured of her illness. She thought she could slip away without anyone knowing what had happened. But she did not understand the nature of Jesus' healing power.

Jesus felt within Himself that healing virtue had gone out of Him, and He turned about in the throng and said, "Who touched my clothing?" The disciples thought this an absurd question, seeing that the people thronged on every side. But the woman, in fear and trembling, knowing what Jesus had done for her, came to Him and knelt at His feet, and told Him the whole truth. Then the Good Physician lovingly said to her, "Daughter, your faith has made you well; go in peace, and be cured of your illness."

While Jesus was still speaking to this woman, and while Jairus was anxiously waiting for Jesus to move on, a messenger came from Jairus' house with bad news, saying, "Your daughter is dead; do not trouble the Master any more." But Jesus, on hearing this, comforted Jairus by saying, "Do not be afraid; only believe, and she shall be well."

And when Jesus came to the house, He permitted no one to enter with Him except Peter and John and James, and the father and mother of the little girl. Jesus said to the crowd of <u>mourners</u> who were weeping and wailing loudly, "Do not weep; for she is not dead but sleeping." But they laughed scornfully at Him, knowing that she was already dead.

people sad because of death

Jesus put them all out of the house, and taking the child's parents and the three disciples went into the room where the beautiful little girl lay, still and white. Jesus took the little girl's hand into His own, and said to her in His own native <u>Aramaic</u> tongue, "*Talitha cumi,*" which means "Little maid, I say to you, 'Arise.' " And instantly the child got up and walked; for she was twelve years old. The parents were beside themselves with joy and astonishment at the recovery of their daughter. Jesus reminded them to give the little girl something to eat, for she was alive and well and hungry again. He also strictly charged them not to tell what He had done, for He wanted the people to know that His

a language spoken in Bible times

real work was to teach the truths of God's kingdom, and to give new life to the souls of men.

# A Lad's Lunch
# and a Great Miracle

*Matthew 14:13–21; Mark 6:30–44; Luke 9:10–17; John 6:1–14*

THE disciples, having buried their friend John the Baptist, returned to Jesus and told Him all about their sad experience. Seeing that His disciples were weary and disheartened, Jesus gently said to them, "Come with me and we will go away to some quiet place and rest awhile." For many were coming and going, and they had no free time even to eat. So they all got into a boat and headed for a lonely spot on the northern shore of a lake, in the region of Bethsaida.

But the crowds of people saw them leave, guessed where they were going, and hurried to the place ahead of them. As Jesus stepped out of the boat, He saw a great crowd of people there to meet Him. Instead of being impatient with them, however, Jesus was moved by compassion for them, because they were like sheep without a shepherd. So again He spent the day, weary as He was, teaching them the truths of the Kingdom, and healing those who were sick.

a feeling of understanding for others

9

Late afternoon came, and the people showed no signs of leaving. The disciples came to Jesus, reminded Him of the lateness of the hour, and urged Him to send the people away into the country and villages round about so that they might buy themselves some food. Jesus surprised and startled them by saying, "You give them some food to eat." But they quickly replied, "We do not have enough money to buy bread for this great number of people, even to give each one a little." Jesus calmly said to them, "How many loaves do you have? Go and see."

At this moment, Andrew spoke up and said, "There is a lad here who has five barley loaves and two small fish; but what are these among so many?" Jesus answered Andrew's question by saying, "Direct the people to sit down." The disciples proceeded to have all the people sit down in groups upon the green grass. So they sat down, by hundreds and by fifties, and with their garments of many bright colors they looked like plots in a vast flower garden. As they waited, their eyes were all fixed upon the scene of the young lad handing his lunch of loaves and fish over to Jesus.

very large

Jesus took the loaves and fish into His hands, lifted His eyes to heaven in a prayer of thanksgiving, blessed the lad's simple offering, broke the loaves into pieces, and gave them to the twelve disciples to set before the people; in like manner He divided the two

*Jesus gave the broken loaves to the disciples to set before the people*

fish among them all. And all the men, women, and children in the vast throng ate of the loaves and fish until their hunger was abated. And the number of those who ate of the loaves and fish was five thousand men, besides the women and children.

When they had all eaten as much as they wanted, Jesus commanded His disciples, saying, "Gather up the broken pieces that are left, so that nothing may be lost." So the disciples gathered them up and filled twelve baskets with the fragments from the five barley loaves and the two fish which remained after the people had eaten.

When the people realized what a wonderful miracle Jesus had performed to care for their needs, they exclaimed, "This is truly the prophet that has come into the world." The happiest person in all that crowd of people was the little lad who had given his lunch to Jesus, that He might use it to feed them.

Following the miracle of the feeding of the five thousand, Jesus returned to Capernaum, and talked there to the people about the deeper meaning of what He had done. He told them that the physical bread which they had eaten was the symbol of the spiritual bread which He came into the world to bring. He urged them to seek for this, which He was able to give them. This is what Jesus said: "I am the bread of life; he that comes to me shall never hunger, and he that believes in me shall never thirst."

# Jesus' Glory
# on the Holy Mount

*Matthew 17:1–8; Mark 9:2–8; Luke 9:28–36*

THE Transfiguration of Jesus took place about a week after Peter had confessed Jesus to be "the Christ, the Son of the living God," at Caesarea Philippi. At this time, Jesus took with Him three of His disciples, Peter, James, and John his brother, and he led them up into a high mountain to pray.

*a change in form and looks*

As Jesus was praying, suddenly a most remarkable change came over Him. His face began to shine as bright as the sun and His garments became sparkling white. The drowsy disciples became fully awake and saw their Master with all the radiant glory shining forth from him.

*shining brightly*

But that was not all. As the disciples watched, suddenly there appeared in this flood of glory two men from the unseen world whom they knew to be Moses and Elijah. These two great servants of God talked with Jesus about His coming death on the cross at Jerusalem.

As Moses and Elijah were departing, Peter

13

said to Jesus, "Master, it is good for us to be here. Let us build three tabernacles, one for you and one for Moses and one for Elijah, so that they can stay with you here a while longer." Peter did not know what he was saying, because he did not understand the meaning of these strange events. But while Peter was still speaking, a bright and luminous cloud came over them all, and it frightened them. To add to the wonder of it all, a heavenly voice came out of the cloud, saying, "This is my beloved Son, with whom I am well pleased; listen to him."

When the three disciples heard this voice, they were overcome with fear and fell to the ground and buried their faces in their arms. Presently Jesus came to them and touched them tenderly and said, "Arise, and do not be afraid." And when the disciples looked up, Moses and Elijah had disappeared, and they saw no one but Jesus.

The three disciples never forgot this experience. John later wrote in his Gospel, "We beheld his glory, the glory as of the only begotten of the Father, full of grace and truth." And Peter wrote, "We were eyewitnesses of His majesty. For He received from God the Father honor and glory, when there came the voice to him from the excellent glory, saying, 'This is my beloved Son, with whom I am well pleased.' And this voice which came from heaven we heard, when we were with him in the holy mount."

brought to life (son)

mountain or hill

14

# Jesus' Parable
# of the Good Samaritan

*Luke 10:25–37*

THE Parable of the Good Samaritan is one of the most familiar stories that Jesus told. The occasion on which Jesus spoke the parable was this. A certain lawyer or scribe came to Jesus one day and asked Him a difficult question. The lawyer was a man trained to interpret and teach the law of Moses to the people. He really felt that he did not need any instruction from Jesus, but he asked the question for the purpose of puzzling and testing Jesus. The question the lawyer asked was this: "Master, what shall I do to inherit eternal life?"

Jesus thought He would let the man answer his own question, so He replied, "What is written in the law of Moses? What do you read there?" This was an easy question for the lawyer, and he readily answered, " 'Thou shalt love the Lord thy God with all thy heart, and with all thy soul, and with all thy strength, and with all thy mind; and thy neighbor as thyself.' " That was a very wise answer, and Jesus said to the man, "You have given the

*short story that teaches a religious truth*

*a writer or teacher of Jewish law*

15

carried out as
promised

right answer; do this, and you will find eternal life."

The reply of Jesus stung the lawyer's conscience. He realized that he had not <u>fulfilled</u> this great commandment of the Law which he could repeat so well. So he attempted to excuse himself for his failure by asking Jesus another question: "And who is my neighbor?" Then Jesus related the following story which showed the lawyer, and which is meant to show anyone else who hears or reads it, what it means to be a good neighbor to one's fellow men.

One day a certain man was going down the lonely and dangerous road from Jerusalem to Jericho. Suddenly a band of thieves sprang upon him, stripped off his clothing, attacked him with clubs, and ran away with all his belongings, leaving the poor man half dead by the roadside.

The man lay there wounded and helpless. Presently a priest, having finished his religious duties in Jerusalem, came down the road and saw the wounded man in his desperate plight. But not wishing to be delayed on his journey, he gave a quick glance at the helpless man and passed by on the other side of the road. A little later a Levite, another religious man whose duty it was to help the priests in the temple service, came by; but he also hurried along without stopping to help.

people living
in Samaria, not
pure Jews

But by and by a <u>Samaritan</u> came riding

16

*The Samaritan eased his wounds*

along, and when he saw the wounded, half-dead man, had compassion for him, and quickly went to him and gave him first aid, using oil and wine to ease his wounds. Then he lifted the suffering man on his own beast, and walking beside him took him to a roadside inn not far away. He stayed with the man all night, caring for him as best he could.

The next morning, as he had to go on his way, he gave the keeper of the inn a sum of money and asked him to take care of the wounded man until he was well again. He assured the innkeeper that he would repay him any additional amount he might have to spend for the man's care when he returned.

When he had finished telling the story, Jesus said to the lawyer, "Now which of these three men, do you think, was a neighbor to the man who fell among the thieves?" The lawyer answered, "The one who showed mercy on him and helped him." Then Jesus said to him, "Go and do likewise."

kindness, greater than usually expected

# The Parable
# of the Prodigal Son

*Luke 15:11–24, 32*

JESUS the friend of sinners was teaching one day when a crowd of tax collectors and those whom the Pharisees called "sinners" drew near to hear Him. The Pharisees and scribes complained about Jesus' friendly attitude toward these outcasts and criticized Him openly, saying, "This man receives sinners and eats with them."

Jesus took this occasion to speak several parables which teach that God is a loving heavenly Father who forgives and restores the penitent sinner who seeks His pardon and mercy. The Parables of the Lost Sheep, the Lost Coin, and the Lost Son all tell how the loving heavenly Father yearns after His wayward children until they are safe in His care and keeping.

The Parable of the Prodigal Son is a profoundly human and moving story. A certain man had two sons; and the younger of them willfully and foolishly said to his father, "Father, give me the portion of your estate that belongs to me." The father, knowing that it

wasteful with money and other things

everything a person owns

was not the wisest thing to do, nevertheless divided his money equally between his two sons.

Very soon thereafter, the younger son gathered together all he had and journeyed into a far country, where he proceeded to spend his substance wastefully in <u>riotous</u> living. Almost before he knew it, he had spent everything he had, and he began to be in want of food, clothing, and shelter. His fair-weather friends all deserted him, and no one helped him in his distress.

*in a wild way*

Out of <u>dire</u> necessity he went to work for one of the men of that country, who sent him into his fields to feed his pigs. The wretched young man was so hungry that he even ate the husks intended for the pigs, as no one gave him any food.

*dreadful*

At last, in his sad and pitiful condition, the prodigal son began to think of the good home he had left and of his kind and loving father. He realized how foolish he had been to leave all this behind. He knew that even his father's hired servants had plenty to eat and to spare, while he was starving in a pigsty far from home. As he was thinking thus, he made a very important decision. This is what he said to himself: "I will arise and go to my father, and will say to him, 'Father, I have sinned against heaven and before you, and I am no longer worthy of being called your son; treat me therefore as one of your hired servants.'"

*The father's heart was filled with love and joy as he met his son*

And he started out at once to return to his father's home. But while he was yet a great way off, his father saw him coming; for he had been looking and longing every day for his boy's return. The old father's heart was filled with love and joy as he ran out to meet his son. Lovingly and tenderly he hugged him and kissed him. The tearful boy knelt at his father's feet and confessed, "Father, I have sinned against heaven and before you, and am no longer worthy of being called your son."

deserving or good enough

But he got no further. His father had already forgiven his penitent son, and he called out to his servants, "Bring forth the best robe and put it on him, and put a ring on his hand and shoes on his feet, and bring the fatted calf here and kill it, and let us eat and be merry; for this my son was dead and is alive again: he was lost and is found." And the whole household began to have a happy and joyful time.

The father gave his poor, ragged boy a royal welcome. He bestowed upon his hungry-hearted son all the love and tenderness of which his fatherly heart was capable. That, said Jesus, is the love and mercy which God gives to the heavenly Father bestows upon each of His penitent, obedient children who returns to the Father's home.

# Jesus the Friend of Children

*Matthew 18:1–6, 10, 14, 19:13–15; Mark 9:*
*33–37, 10:13–16; Luke 9:46–48, 18:15–17*

THE Gospel stories give two beautiful glimpses of Jesus as the friend
of little children. The first scene is
in a house in Capernaum; the sec-
ond is by the wayside in Perea. These scenes,
though few, are precious to the hearts of
Christians the world over, because they tell
about the Saviour who loves the children of
all lands and races; about the Good Shepherd
who gathers the lambs in His arms, and car-
ries them in His bosom.

Soon after Jesus was glorified on the Holy
Mount, He returned with His disciples to the
city of Capernaum. On the way the disciples
began to argue and quarrel among themselves as to which one of them was the greatest. Jesus heard them arguing, and decided
they needed to be taught a lesson that would
make them more humble and kind and un-
selfish.

So when they came into a certain house in
Capernaum (some think it was Peter's house),
Jesus asked the disciples, "What were you ar-

first four books of
the New Testament

23

guing about on the way?" They all kept still, because they felt guilty that they had quarreled with one another. Jesus sat down in the house and called the twelve to gather around Him. Then He quietly said to them, "If any one of you wants to be first, he must be last of all and servant of all." By this Jesus meant that the way of humble service is the way to true greatness. Then, wishing to give them an object lesson they would never forget, He called a little child to Him (he may have been Peter's own little boy), and put him in the midst of the disciples. He took the child in His arms and said to the twelve, "Whoever receives one such child in my name, receives me; and whoever receives me, receives not only me but also the Father who sent me."

Then Jesus added, "Truly I say to you, unless you change and become like little children, you will not enter the kingdom of heaven. Whoever humbles himself like this child, he is the greatest in the kingdom of heaven. Whoever offends one of these little ones who believe in me, it would be better for him to have a great <u>millstone</u> hung around his neck and to be drowned in the depth of the sea." Then the Master concluded, "Be sure you do not despise one of these little ones; for I say to you that in heaven their angels always behold the face of my Father who is in heaven. Moreover, it is not the will of your Father who is in heaven that one of these lit-

large flat stone used to grind grain

*Jesus took the little children into His loving arms*

die

scolded in a
sharp way

tle ones should perish." The disciples were very much humbled by this lesson, and tried to be more loving and kind to one another.

Some time later, on His last journey toward Jerusalem, Jesus came one day to a quiet and pleasant place in Perea, east of the Jordan. As He stopped there to rest and to teach the people, a number of young mothers brought their little children to Him, so that He might touch them and bless them. But the disciples rebuked these parents and tried to send them away. They evidently thought that Jesus was too busy to pay any attention to the children. But they were wrong.

Jesus was highly displeased with what the disciples were doing, and said to them, "Let the little children come to me, and do not send them away; for to the childlike belongs the kingdom of God." Then He said to all the people, "Truly I say to you, anyone among you who does not receive the kingdom of God like a little child shall not enter it." And Jesus took the little children into His loving arms and blessed them, caressing their heads with His gentle hands.

# Jesus the Good Shepherd

*John 10:1–18*

AFTER He had healed and received the man who had been born blind, Jesus taught the people in Jerusalem the beautiful allegory of the Sheepfold and the Good Shepherd. He did this to rebuke the Pharisees for having cast out the poor man to whom Jesus had given sight; to encourage the man in his faith and trust; and to describe again the loving, saving ministry of the Son of man who came to give His life as a ransom for many.

*a story that teaches something special*

It has been said that this story in John's Gospel is the New Testament version of the Twenty-third Psalm, the "Shepherd Psalm." David, a faithful shepherd himself, sang, "The Lord is my shepherd"; and Jesus, who was called "the Son of David," claimed to be the True Shepherd whom God sent to seek and to save the lost sheep.

The first scene is in the early morning when the sheep are being led out from the fold by the shepherd. Jesus said, "Truly I say to you, anyone who does not enter the sheepfold by the door, but gets in by climbing over the wall, that man is a thief and a robber. But the one who comes in by the door is the real shepherd of the sheep. The doorkeeper opens the door to him; the sheep hear and know his voice, and he calls his own sheep by name and leads them out to find pasture. When he has led out all his own sheep, he walks in front of them, and the sheep follow him, for they know his voice. The sheep will not follow a stranger, but will run away from him, because they do not know the stranger's voice."

The people did not understand this too well, so Jesus tried to make it plainer to them. He said to them again, "Truly I say to you, I am the door of the sheep. Those who have come before me and claimed to be the way to God have been thieves and robbers, but listen to God's people did not <u>heed</u> them. I only am the true door into the sheepfold; and anyone who enters through me will be saved, and will freely go in and out and find pasture.

"The thief comes to the fold only to steal and to kill and to destroy the sheep. But I came so that the sheep may have life, and have it abundantly. I am the good shepherd. The good shepherd is willing to lay down his life for the sheep. But one who serves only for hire, and who does not own or care for the sheep, when he sees the wolf coming, runs away and leaves the sheep, and permits the wolf to seize and scatter them. Again I say, I

*Jesus the Good Shepherd*

am the good shepherd. I know my own sheep and they know me, just as the Father knows me and I know the Father. Knowing the needs of my sheep in this way, I am willing to lay down my life for them.

God's chosen people, Israelites

"And I have other sheep beside and beyond the fold of Israel, even the people of all nations. I must bring them into the fold also, and they will hear my voice. And there shall be one fold, and one shepherd.

"This is the reason the Father loves me as He does, because I lay down my life for all the sheep. No man can take my life from me, but I lay it down of my own will. I have power to lay it down, and I have power to take it up again. This commandment I have received from my Father, and I must obey His will."

By this Jesus meant that as the Good Shepherd He would lay down His life as a sacrifice upon the cross, and that He would take up His life again by way of His resurrection from the grave. All who believe in Him as the Saviour and Lord belong to the "one fold" of which He is the "one shepherd."

# Jesus Raises His Friend Lazarus

*John 11:1–44*

JOHN, in his Gospel, records only seven of the signs or miracles of Jesus, and the last and greatest of all is the raising of Lazarus from the grave. Lazarus was the brother of Mary and Martha whose home was in <u>Bethany</u>. They were all dear friends of Jesus, and the Master often visited their home where He received a warm welcome and loving care.

a small town near Jerusalem

One day when Jesus was a day's journey away from Bethany, in the region east of the Jordan, Lazarus became very sick. Mary and Martha were greatly concerned about their brother, and they hastily sent a messenger to Jesus with the word, "Lord, he whom you love is sick." They knew that Jesus would be able to help them in their trouble. When Jesus received the message, He said to His disciples, "This sickness is not to death; but for the glory of God, so that the Son of God may be glorified by it." But for some mysterious reason, Jesus stayed two days longer in the place where He was.

Then after that He said to the disciples,

"Let us go back to Judea again." The disciples tried to persuade Jesus not to go, because they were afraid of what His enemies might do to Him. But Jesus <u>reassured</u> them by saying that God would take care of Him as long as He was doing the Father's work and will. Then He explained to the disciples what He was going to do. "Our friend Lazarus," He said, "is sleeping, but I am going so that I may awaken him out of his sleep." The disciples thought Jesus meant that Lazarus was taking rest in sleep, and said, "Master, if he is only sleeping, he will get well." Then Jesus told them plainly, "Lazarus is dead." And He added, "I am glad for your sake that I was not there, so that you may believe. Now let us go to him."

So when Jesus came to Bethany, He found that Lazarus had lain in the grave four days. As soon as Martha heard that Jesus was coming, she hurried forth to meet Him, but Mary remained in the house. Martha immediately unburdened her heart to Jesus, saying, "Lord, if you had been here my brother would not have died. But I know that even now God will give you whatever you ask." Jesus consoled Martha by saying, "Your brother shall rise again." Martha replied, "Yes, I know he will rise again in the <u>resurrection</u> at the last day," but she was not fully comforted. Then Jesus spoke to her these great words of promise and hope, saying, "I am the resurrection

told or promised again

coming back to life after death

*Before the astonished gaze of all, Lazarus came forth*

and the life; he that believes in me, though he were dead, yet shall he live; and whoever lives and believes in me shall never die. Do you believe this?" Martha humbly replied, "Yes, Lord; I believe that you are the Christ, the Son of God, who should come into the world."

When Martha had said this, she went into the house and softly called her sister Mary, saying, "The Master has come and is calling for you." Mary rose quickly and went to Jesus. When she came where Jesus was and saw Him, she fell at His feet, saying to Him the same words that Martha had spoken: "Lord, if you had been here my brother would not have died." When Jesus saw Mary weeping, and her Jewish friends weeping with her, His spirit was moved and He was troubled, and He asked, "Where have you laid him?" They said to Him, "Lord, come and see." And Jesus wept with Mary.

Then Jesus, His spirit again moved, came to the grave where Lazarus was buried. It was a cave, and a great stone covered the opening. Jesus commanded those who stood by, "Take away the stone." But Martha would have prevented them, saying to Jesus, "Lord, by this time his body will be decaying, for he has been dead four days." But Jesus reminded her, "Did I not just tell you that if you would

power and splendor only believe you would see the <u>glory</u> of God?"

So they took away the stone. And Jesus

34

lifted up His eyes and prayed, saying, "Father, I thank you for hearing me. And I knew that you hear me always; but because of the people who are standing by I said it, so that they may believe that you sent me." When He had thus prayed, He called with a loud voice, "Lazarus, come forth." And before the astonished gaze of all, the dead man came forth, bound hand and foot with grave clothes, and his face bound about with a napkin. Jesus said to those who stood near, "Untie him and let him go." So Lazarus was alive once more and was restored to his sisters Mary and Martha, to live with them in their happy home.

# Jesus Anointed
# by Mary of Bethany

*Matthew 26:1–13; Mark 14:1–9; John 12:1–8*

THE anointing of Jesus by Mary of Bethany has been called one of the most beautiful acts of love and devotion ever bestowed upon the Saviour. It shows what one of the loving friends of Jesus did for Him at a time when the chief priests and scribes were plotting to kill Him, and when Judas Iscariot was conspiring to betray Him.

Jewish holiday in memory of being freed from slavery in Egypt

Six days before the <u>Passover,</u> that is, on the day before Palm Sunday, Jesus came to Bethany and lodged in the home of His friend Simon the leper. Some time before this, Jesus had evidently cured this man of his leprosy, and Simon had become a follower of Jesus. Simon may have been a relative of Mary, Martha, and Lazarus, or possibly the husband of Martha. These friends at Bethany made a supper in honor of Jesus and in gratitude to Him for having raised Lazarus from the dead. Lazarus was there and Martha helped serve the fine supper.

While the meal was in progress, and the

guests were reclining on couches around the table, Mary quietly entered the room with an alabaster box of ointment in her hand and stood beside Jesus. Breaking the alabaster box of precious and costly ointment of nard, she poured it lavishly upon the head of Jesus and also anointed His feet with the fragrant perfume. Then, unbinding her long tresses, she wiped the Master's feet with her hair. And the house was filled with the sweet smell of the ointment.

The disciples watched all this but did not approve of what Mary had done. They became indignant and began to criticize and find fault with Mary. They complained against her, saying, "Why was the ointment wasted in this way? For it might have been sold for more than three hundred pence, and the money given to the poor." And they spoke very unkindly to poor Mary. In all this unseemly conduct, Judas Iscariot, who was to betray Jesus for thirty pieces of silver, was the ringleader. John, the disciple whom Jesus loved, says that Judas spoke as he did, not because he cared for the poor but because he was a thief, and that he even stole money out of the bag which belonged to the disciples.

But Jesus rebuked these selfish men and put a stop to their ugly and unkind words, saying, "Let her alone; why do you want to trouble her?" He then commended Mary for her loving deed, saying, "She has done a very good

smooth white stone that can be carved

sweet smelling oil

thing for me." Then reminding these thought-less men of His approaching sufferings and death, He solemnly said to them, "You will always have the poor with you, and you can do good to them whenever you wish; but you will not always have me."

Jesus continued to praise and commend Mary for the loving desire and wise perception that had led her to perform her selfless act. "She has done what she could," He said; "she has in reality come beforehand to anoint my body for the burial." Jesus meant that Mary had done not the least but the greatest work she could possibly have done. He thought of her deed as having special relationship to His coming death on the cross.

Jesus concluded His praise and commendation of Mary with a statement concerning the timeless and universal influence of her beautiful deed. These were His words, "Truly I say to you, wherever this gospel is preached throughout the whole world, what she has done will be spoken of as a memorial of her."

in every time and place

39

*Mary of Bethany wiped His feet with her hair*

# Palm Sunday—
# The King's Triumphal Entry

*Matthew 21:1–17; Mark 11:1–11; Luke 19:29–38; John 12:12–18*

ALM Sunday marks the day of the coming of the King. On this day, Jesus made His royal entry into the city of Jerusalem and presented Himself to the people as the Son of David and as the King of Israel.

On His last journey to Jerusalem, Jesus finally came, with His disciples, to the villages of Bethany and Bethphage, on the Mount of Olives, just east of Jerusalem. Here He made preparations for His dramatic entrance into the city. He sent two of His disciples, who are not named, saying to them, "Go into the next village, and you will at once find an ass tied and a colt with her. Free them and bring them to me. If anyone says anything to you, you shall say, 'The Lord has need of them.'" So those who were sent went to the village and found it as Jesus had said. As they were freeing the colt, its owners said to them, "Why are you freeing the colt?" The disciples replied, "The Lord has need of it."

Matthew notes that the manner in which Jesus planned His triumphal entry into Jerusalem was an exact fulfillment of the word spoken by the prophet Zechariah, saying:

"Tell ye the daughter of Zion,
  Behold, thy King cometh unto thee,
  Meek, and riding upon an ass,
  And upon a colt the foal of an ass."

The disciples quickly brought the colt to Jesus, as He had directed. Then some of the disciples put their garments on the back of the colt to form a cushion, and Jesus sat thereon. As the lowly procession started down the slope of the Mount of Olives, most of the crowd of happy pilgrims spread their garments on the road for Jesus to ride over. Others of the multitude cut branches from the palm trees and scattered them on the road. And the throngs of people that went before Him and that followed after shouted, "Hosanna to the Son of David! Blessed is he who comes in the name of the Lord! Hosanna in the highest!" This was a familiar prayer to God for deliverance based on the words of Psalm 118:25–26. The word Hosanna means "save, we pray."

a shout of praise to God

When the colorful procession with King Jesus at the head entered Jerusalem, all the city was deeply roused, and the people kept asking, "Who is this?" Some of the people in the crowd answered, "This is Jesus the prophet from Nazareth of Galilee."

41

And it came to pass that Jesus went into the temple of God and put out all those who sold and bought in the temple, and threw over the tables of the money-changers and the seats of those who sold doves. He rebuked these evildoers, saying to them, "It is written, 'My house shall be called the house of prayer; but you have made it a den of thieves.'"

Then the blind and the lame came to Him in the temple, and He healed them. But when the chief priests and the scribes saw the wonderful things that He did, and when they heard the children shouting in the temple, "Hosanna to the Son of David!" they were very angry, and said to Him, "Do you hear what these children are saying?" And Jesus said to them, "Yes. Have you never read the Scriptures which say, 'Out of the mouth of babes and sucklings you have perfected praise'?" And leaving these hard-hearted men, Jesus went out of the city and returned to Bethany to find lodging with His friends.

*WORLD'S BIBLE STORY LIBRARY*

those who changed odd money into the kind used in the temple

*The procession entered Jerusalem*

# The Last Supper
# in the Upper Room

*Matthew 26:17–29; Mark 14:12–25; Luke 22:7–23; John 13:1–15*

THE Feast of the Passover was insti- tuted by Moses to commemorate the redemption of the Israelites from their bondage in Egypt. It reminded the people that when the first-born of the Egyptians were slain, the houses of the Israel- ites, where the blood of lambs had been sprin- kled, were passed over by the angel of death. The Passover feast began with a sacrificial meal. A lamb was slain in the early evening, roasted whole, and eaten with unleavened bread and bitter herbs. This Passover had been kept by the Israelites from the time of Moses until the time of Jesus. The story of how this ancient Passover was fulfilled and how Jesus gave it a new meaning, so far as Christians are concerned, is told in the ac- count of the institution of the Lord's Supper.

During the last week of His life (now called Holy Week) Jesus spent every day teaching in the temple, and at night He went out and lodged with His friends at Bethany. The Day of Unleavened Bread, or the Feast

*to keep alive in the memory*

*having to do with special offerings*

45

*Judas left Jesus and the eleven loyal disciples at the Last Supper* of the Passover, came on Thursday of that week. On this day the lamb for the Passover feast was killed and eaten.

When this sacred day came, Jesus sent the two disciples Peter and John, saying, "Go and prepare the Passover for us, so that we may eat it together." The disciples asked, "Where do you want us to prepare it?" Jesus answered, "Behold, when you have entered the city, a man will meet you there carrying a pitcher of water. Follow him into the house which he enters, and say to the owner of the house, 'The Master says to you, "Where is the guest room where I shall eat the Passover with my disciples?" ' And this man will show you a large upper room furnished; there make ready." The two disciples carried out these instructions, and found it just as Jesus had told them. And they made ready the Passover.

room on second floor or roof used for guests and special affairs

Now when evening came, Jesus came into the house and went up to the large upper room, where they found the Passover supper all ready. Jesus sat at the center of the table, and the twelve apostles took their places around Him. In earnest tones the Master said to them, "I have greatly desired to eat this Passover with you before I suffer; for I tell you I shall never eat it again until it is fulfilled in the kingdom of God." And as they were eating, Jesus became very sad and sorrowful and said, "Truly I say to you, one of you will betray me." And they too became

turn against

46

sorrowful, and began to say to Him one after another, "Is it I, Lord?" Jesus answered, "It is one of the twelve, even one who is dipping bread in the same dish with me." He then added this solemn warning, "The Son of man indeed goes as it is written of him, but woe to that man by whom the Son of man is betrayed! That man would have been better off never to have been born." Judas, who was to betray Him, said, "Master, is it I?" Jesus replied to the guilty man, "You have said it." And Judas went out into the darkness of night.

As Jesus continued eating, with the eleven loyal disciples around Him, He took bread, and when He had blessed it, He broke it and said, "Take, eat; this is my body." And He took a cup, and when He had given thanks He gave it to them, and they all drank of it. He explained the meaning of what they were doing by saying, "This is my blood of the new testament, which is shed for many for the remission of sins." He was referring to His coming death on the cross, as the Lamb of God who takes away the sin of the world. Then He added this promise, "I tell you I shall not drink again of this fruit of the vine until that day when I drink it new with you in my Father's kingdom."

forgiveness

John's account of the Last Supper relates how, after supper was over, Jesus rose from the table, laid aside His upper garments, and took a towel and wrapped it around Himself. Then He poured water into a basin and began to wash the disciples' feet, and to wipe them with the towel with which He was wrapped. He came to Simon Peter, and Peter objected, saying, "Lord, are you washing my feet?" Jesus replied, "What I do you do not know now, but you shall know later." But Peter foolishly retorted, "You shall never wash my feet." Jesus answered him, "If I do not wash you, you have no part with me." Then Peter, ashamed and humbled, replied, "Lord, not my feet only, but also my hands and my head."

When Jesus had washed their feet, and taken His garments and sat down again at the table, He explained the meaning of what He had done to them, saying, "You call me Master and Lord; and you speak rightly, for so I am. If I then, your Lord and Master, have washed your feet, you also ought to wash one another's feet. For I have given you an example, and you should do as I have done to you."

So the Lord's Supper was instituted by Jesus. It is the memorial of the Saviour's <u>aton-</u>

making up for something

<u>ing</u> death on the cross. The bread is the symbol of His broken body. The cup is the symbol of His shed blood. The Lord's Supper is observed because Jesus said, "This do in remembrance of me."

48

# The Saviour's Prayer in Gethsemane

*Matthew 26:36–46; Mark 14:32–42; Luke 22:39–46*

THE Garden of Gethsemane is remembered as the scene of the agony, great suffering the betrayal, and the arrest of the Lord Jesus. The name Gethsemane means "Oil press," and indicates that it was a garden of olive trees with an oil press for pressing oil out of the olives. The garden was situated on the western slope of the Mount of Olives, east of Jerusalem, across the brook Kidron. Gethsemane was a favorite sanctuary of prayer for Jesus when He was in that vicinity. He evidently went there again and again to pray, after His busy days of teaching and ministering in Jerusalem. For Luke says, "And he came out, and went, as was his habit, to the Mount of Olives."

Jesus and the eleven faithful disciples concluded their fellowship in the upper room with the singing of a hymn. The Master led the way through the deepening shadows to the Mount of Olives, and the disciples followed. When they came to the garden, Jesus stationed eight of the disciples at the entrance to keep watch,

49

saying, "Sit down here while I go over there and pray."

Taking with Him Peter and the two sons of Zebedee, James and John, He went into the recesses of the garden. The Master began to be very sorrowful and heavy-hearted, and said to the three disciples, "My soul is exceedingly sorrowful, even to death; stay here and watch with me." The disciples were very tired and troubled, and did not seem to understand what the Master expected of them.

Jesus went a little farther into the depths of the garden and knelt down and prayed most earnestly, saying, "Father, if you are willing, remove this cup from me; nevertheless not my will, but yours, be done." Jesus was referring to the "cup" of His sufferings and death on the cross as the Bearer of the sins of the world. Although Jesus, in His human nature, shrank from the ordeal that lay ahead, yet as the Son of man and Son of God He submitted Himself wholly to do the Father's will.

Then He rose up from His prayer and came to the three disciples and found them sleeping. He said to Peter, "Simon, are you asleep? Could you not watch one hour? Watch and pray lest you enter into temptation; the spirit truly is willing but the flesh is weak." Again He went away, praying the same words a second time. And there appeared to Him an angel from heaven, strengthening Him.

difficult and painful experience

51

*Jesus prayed in the depths of the garden*

followers and
believers in Jesus'
teachings

He returned a second time to the disciples and found them still sleeping, for their eyes were heavy. This time He did not disturb them, but leaving them again went away and prayed for the third time, using the same words. And being in an agony He prayed more earnestly; and His sweat became like great drops of blood falling to the ground.

Then for the third and last time Jesus came to the disciples and said to them, "Why are you still asleep and taking your rest? It is enough; the hour has come; behold, the Son of man is betrayed into the hands of sinners. Rise up, let us go; behold, my betrayer is now at hand." Through the branches of the olive trees, Jesus could see the flaring torches of those who were coming to take Him.

The disciples failed to sympathize and watch with their Master during His hour of agony in Gethsemane, but He did not fail to watch over them. Having loved His own as the Good Shepherd, He loved them to the end.

# The Betrayal
# and Arrest of Jesus

*Matthew 26:47–56, 27:3–5;*
*Mark 14:43–52; Luke 22:47–53; John 18:2–14*

WHEN Jesus had concluded His prayer in Gethsemane, and while He was still speaking to the drowsy disciples, the silence of the garden was shattered by the arrival of a motley throng of people. In this band of rough men were soldiers, captains of the temple, and representatives of the chief priests, scribes, and elders of the people. They were carrying torches and lanterns, and were armed with swords and sticks. Judas was leading the procession, because he knew the place where Jesus often went with His disciples.

The Master, knowing everything that was going to happen to Him, took command of the situation. He went forth out of the shadows of the olive trees and said to the startled company, "Whom do you seek?" They answered Him, "Jesus of Nazareth." Jesus calmly said to them, "I am he." When Jesus said to them, "I am he," and when they beheld His face still marked with the bloody sweat of His agony, they were overcome with

a garden where Jesus prayed

awe and fear, and stepped back and fell to the ground. When they had recovered somewhat, Jesus asked them again, "Whom do you seek?" And they said again, "Jesus of Nazareth." Jesus said, "I have told you that I am he; if therefore you seek me, let these men go their way."

those over other
priests of Hebrew
church

Now Judas had agreed with the chief priests upon a signal, saying, "Whoever I shall kiss is the man; arrest him and lead him away safely." So he drew near to Jesus and said, "Hail, Master," and kissed Him on the cheek. This abuse of the sign of friendship stung the soul of Jesus deeply, and He said to the betrayer, "Judas, do you dare to betray the Son of man with a kiss?"

The band of soldiers then laid rough hands upon Jesus and arrested Him. Then Simon Peter, having a sword, drew it and with a wild blow struck the servant of the high priest, Malchus, and cut off his right ear. But Jesus restrained Peter with the command, "Put your sword into its sheath; shall I not drink the cup which my Father has given me? All who take the sword will perish by the sword. Do you think that I cannot pray to my Father and He will send me more than twelve legions of angels?" And He touched the ear of Malchus and healed him.

Then the Lord turned to the crowd and said, "Have you come out as against a thief with swords and sticks to arrest me? I sat daily with you teaching in the temple and you did not lay hands on me. But now this is your hour, and the power of darkness." He then added, "But all this has come to pass in order that the words of the prophets might be fulfilled."

Then all the disciples forsook their Master and fled. And a young man, some say it was John Mark, followed Jesus as they led Him away. The young man had only a linen cloth about his body, and when the enemies of Jesus tried to seize him, he left the linen cloth in their hands and ran away naked.

left

So the band of soldiers and their captain and the officers of the Jews bound Jesus and led Him away. First they led Him to the house of Annas; for he was the father-in-law of Caiaphas, who was high priest that year. It was this Caiaphas who had given counsel to the Jews that it was expedient that one man should die for the people. So they had conspired to put Jesus to death.

When Judas, who had betrayed Him, saw that Jesus was condemned, he repented and brought back the thirty pieces of silver to the chief priests and the elders, saying, "I have sinned in that I have betrayed the innocent blood." But they haughtily replied, "What is that to us? See to it yourself." And throwing down the pieces of silver on the pavement, Judas went out and hanged himself.

scornfully

# Jesus Before His Judges

highest Jewish court
and council

THERE are two general phases of the trial of Jesus: the ecclesiastical trial before the Jewish sanhedrin, or council, and the civil trial before the Roman governor Pontius Pilate. There are four different stages of the trial, as Jesus was arraigned in turn before Annas, Caiaphas, Pilate, and Herod. The confused and swiftly moving events of that night of trial can best be understood if attention is paid to the various parts of the story in logical order. The trial of Jesus, the innocent Saviour, was an ordeal of indescribable anguish, suffering, and torture.

## JESUS BEFORE ANNAS

*John 18:12–14; 19–24*

FROM the scene of His arrest in the Garden of Gethsemane, the Master was led by His captors to the house of Annas in Jerusalem.

Late in the night, with His hands bound behind His back, Jesus stood before Annas the high priest. The high priest began by asking Jesus questions about His disciples and His teaching. Jesus boldly answered him, "I spoke openly to the world; I always taught in the synagogue and in the temple, where the Jews always go; and I have said nothing in secret. Why do you ask me? Ask those who heard me what I said to them; behold, they know what I said."

Despite this honest and respectful reply, one of the officers standing by struck Jesus with his hand, saying, "Is that the way for you to answer the high priest?" Jesus answered this brutal man, "If I have spoken ill, bear witness to the evil; but if well, why do you hit me?" Annas then sent Jesus bound to Caiaphas the high priest.

## JESUS BEFORE CAIAPHAS

*Matthew 26:57–68; Mark 14:53–65; Luke 22:63–71*

IT WAS about daybreak when Jesus was brought before Caiaphas, in the council chamber, where the chief priests and scribes and elders had hastily gathered together. Now the chief priests and the whole council sought

when it begins to get light in the morning

57

false witnesses against Jesus, so that they might condemn Him to death. Many witnesses came forward and brought false charges against Jesus, but these witnesses did not agree with one another. At last two came forward and falsely accused Him, saying, "We heard him say, 'I will destroy this temple that is made with hands, and within three days I will build another made without hands.'"

Then Caiaphas stood up in the middle of the council and asked Jesus, "Are you not going to answer at all? What is it that these men say against you?" But Jesus kept still and gave no answer. Again the high priest said to Him, "I command you, by the living God, to tell us whether you are the Christ, the Son of God." Jesus replied to Caiaphas, "I am; and you will see the Son of man sitting at the right hand of power, and coming with the clouds of heaven."

Whereupon the high priest tore his robes and exclaimed, "He has spoken blasphemy! Why do we need any further witnesses? You have heard the blasphemy. What is your judgment?" And they all condemned Him as deserving to be put to death.

not showing honor and respect to God

Then some of those present began to spit in the Saviour's face, and to cover His face, and to slap Him. And some of them said to Him in mockery, "Prophesy to us, you Christ! Who is it that struck you?" And the burly guards pounded Him with blows.

# JESUS BEFORE PILATE

*Matthew 27:1–2, 11–14; Mark 15:1–5;
Luke 23:1–5; John 18:28–38*

WHEN morning came, all the chief priests and scribes and elders of the people took counsel together against Jesus to put Him to death. And when they had bound Him they led Him away and delivered Him to Pontius Pilate the Roman governor. It was very early when they came to the hall of judgment. The Jewish rulers themselves did not go into the judgment hall, because they did not want to defile themselves; they wished to be ceremonially clean to eat the Passover.

So Pilate went out to them and said, "What accusation do you bring against this man?" They replied, "If he were not an evildoer we would not have given him over to you." This reply made Pilate angry, and he said, "Take him yourselves then and judge him according to your own law." But the Jews warily replied, "It is not lawful for us to put any man to death." John notes that this statement fulfilled Jesus' prediction that He would die on the cross, not by stoning, which was the Jewish method of putting one to death.

*in a careful and guarded manner*

Then Pilate entered the judgment hall again and called Jesus to him. So Jesus stood before Pontius Pilate. Pilate asked Jesus, "Are you the King of the Jews?" Jesus answered, "Do

you say this yourself, or have you heard others say it about me?" Pilate was irked by this reply, and demanded, "Am I a Jew? Your own nation and the chief priests have given you over to me. What have you done?" Jesus startled Pilate by saying, "My kingdom is not of this world; if my kingdom were of this world, then my servants would fight to prevent me from being given over to the Jews; but now my kingdom is not of this place." With a show of interest Pilate said to Him, "Are you a king then?" Jesus, seeking to win Pilate, responded, "You say that I am a king. To this end I was born, and for this cause I came into the world, that I should bear witness to the truth. Everyone that is of the truth hears my voice." But Pilate turned away, saying, "What is truth?"

Outside the judgment hall again, the chief priests and elders shouted their accusations against Jesus, saying, "We found this man perverting our nation, and forbidding us to give tribute to Caesar, claiming that he himself is Christ a king." But Jesus did not answer their lies. Then Pilate said to Him, "Do you not hear how many things they declare against you?" But Jesus did not answer Pilate either, not even to defend himself against one charge; so that Pilate was astonished.

Pilate silenced the crowd, and announced his verdict, saying, "I find no fault in this man." But they were all the more insistent,

leading away
from what is good
and right

61

*Jesus was again brought before Pilate*

shouting, "He stirs up the people, teaching throughout all Jewry, from Galilee to this very city."

## JESUS BEFORE HEROD

*Luke 23:6–12*

W HEN Pilate heard this, he asked whether the man was a Galilean. And as soon as he heard that Jesus belonged to Herod's jurisdiction, he sent Him over to Herod, who was himself also in Jerusalem at that time. Pilate thus wished to avoid making a decision as to the fate of Jesus, and tried to shift the responsibility to Herod.

the territory under
one's control

So Jesus was brought face to face with Herod Antipas, the man who had put John the Baptist to death, the man Jesus had referred to as "that fox." When Herod saw Jesus, he was very glad, for he had desired to see Him for a long time. He had heard much about Jesus and was hoping to see some miracle performed by Him.

Herod asked Jesus a great many questions, but Jesus gave the wicked king no answer whatever. The chief priests and the scribes had followed Jesus to Herod's palace and they stood near by, vehemently accusing Him. Herod was greatly angered by Jesus' refusal to speak, and decided to punish Him. So Herod and his soldiers treated Him with scorn and insulted Him. Then, in mockery, Herod arrayed Jesus in a gorgeous royal robe and sent Him back to Pilate. And Herod and Pilate became friends that same day, for before they had been at odds with each other.

## JESUS AGAIN BEFORE PILATE

*Matthew 27:15-31; Mark 15:6-20;*
*Luke 23:13-25; John 18:39-19:16*

WHEN Jesus was brought back to Pilate, the latter called together the chief priests, the rulers, and the people, and said to them, "You brought this man to me as one who has been perverting the people; and behold, I examined him before you and found no fault in him touching those matters of which you accuse him; no, nor yet did Herod; for I sent you to him and lo, nothing worthy of death was done to him. I will therefore chastise him and release him."

beat or punish

Now at the time of the Passover it was the custom for the governor to release for the crowd any one prisoner whom they wanted. They had at the time a notorious prisoner, by the name of Barabbas, a man who had been thrown into prison for starting an uprising in the city, and for murder. So when the crowd gathered and presented their request, Pilate said to them, "Whom should I release to you —Barabbas, or Jesus who is called the

63

Christ?" For Pilate knew that it was because of envy that they had brought Jesus before him. Moreover, when he had sat down on the judgment seat, his wife sent word to him, saying, "Do not have anything to do with that righteous man, for I have suffered greatly because of him today in a dream."

But the chief priests and the elders got busy and persuaded the crowd to ask for Barabbas and destroy Jesus. The governor again said to them, "Which of these two should I release to you?" And they cried out, "Barabbas!" Pilate said to them, "What shall I do then with Jesus who is called the Christ?" They all shouted out, "Let him be crucified!" A third time he said to them, "Why, what evil has he done?" But they cried out all the more, "Crucify, crucify him!" And their voices won out.

So when Pilate saw that he could not prevail, but rather that a commotion was starting, he took a basin of water and washed his hands before the throng, saying, "I am innocent of the blood of this righteous man; see to it yourselves." And all the people answered, accepting the responsibility for Jesus' death, "Let his blood be on us, and on our children." So Pilate gave sentence that their demand be granted. Then he released Barabbas to them, whipped and having scourged Jesus, delivered Him to be crucified.

John's account supplies other details of this picture. The soldiers, John says, wove a crown of thorns and put it on Jesus' head, and put a purple robe on Him, and mocked Him, saying, "Hail, King of the Jews!" And they struck Him with their hands.

Pilate went out again and said to the people, "Behold, I am about to bring him out to you, that you may know that I find no fault in him." Then Jesus came out, wearing the crown of thorns and the purple robe. Pilate said to them, "Behold the man!" When the chief priests and the officers saw Him, they cried out, "Crucify him, crucify him!"

to kill by hanging on a cross

Pilate replied, "Take him yourselves and crucify him, for I do not find any fault in him." The Jews responded, "We have a law, and by our law he ought to die, because he made himself the Son of God." When Pilate heard these words, he was very much afraid. And going into the judgment hall again, he said to Jesus, "Where are you from?" But Jesus gave him no answer. Pilate therefore said to Him, "You refuse to speak to me? Are you not aware that I have power to crucify you and power to release you?" Jesus calmly answered him, "You could have no power at all over me unless it had been given you from above; therefore the one who delivered me to you has the greater sin."

Then Pilate sought to release Jesus, but the Jews cried out, "If you set this man free, you are not Caesar's friend; whoever makes himself a king speaks against Caesar." When Pilate heard these words, he brought Jesus out and sat down on the judgment seat at a place called the Pavement.

Now it was the day of preparation for the Passover. It was about the sixth hour, or noon. Pilate said to the Jews, "Behold your King!" But they cried out, "Away with him, away with him, crucify him!" Pilate said to them, "Shall I crucify your King?" The chief priests answered, "We have no king but Caesar." Then Pilate gave Jesus over to be crucified.

# The Crucifixion of Jesus

T HE story of the trial of Jesus begins with His falling into the hands of His enemies at the time of His arrest in Gethsemane. The story of the crucifixion and death of Jesus begins with His being handed over to His executioners after Pilate had scourged Him.

persons in charge of putting to death

## THE SOLDIERS MOCK JESUS

*Matthew 27:27–31; Mark 15:16–20*

T HE soldiers of the Roman governor took Jesus into the judgment hall, and they gathered the whole company of soldiers before Him. They stripped off His outer garments and put a scarlet robe on Him. They plaited a crown of thorns and put it on His head, and put a reed in His right hand. And they knelt before Him and mocked Him, shouting, "Hail, King of the Jews!" And they spat upon Him, and took the reed out of His hand, and struck Him on the head. And after they had thus mocked Him, they took the scarlet robe off him, put His own garments on Him again, and led Him away to crucify Him.

## SIMON CARRIES THE CROSS FOR JESUS

*Matthew 27:32; Mark 15:21; Luke 23:26*

As they were leading Jesus away, they met a man by the name of Simon, from Cyrene, a city in North Africa, who was coming into Jerusalem from the country. So far Jesus had been carrying His own cross. But the soldiers laid rough hands on Simon, put the cross on his back, and compelled him to carry it after Jesus. Simon became a follower of Jesus, for Mark tells us that he was the father of Alexander and Rufus, two young men who were well known to the early Christian community.

## THE WEEPING DAUGHTERS OF JERUSALEM

*Luke 23:27–31*

As Jesus was conducted by the Roman soldiers on their journey to Golgotha, a very large crowd of people followed Him. In this company were a number of young women of Jerusalem who were truly sorry for the Galilean, and who bewailed and <u>lamented</u> Him.

cried or complained
because of sorrow

For this they are often referred to as "the weeping daughters of Jerusalem." The Master noticed these kind friends, and was comforted by their expression of sympathy.

Turning to them the compassionate Saviour said, "Daughters of Jerusalem, do not weep for me, but weep rather for yourselves and for your children. For behold, the days are coming when they will say, 'Blessed are those who never bore or nurtured children.'

"At that time they will begin to say to the mountains, 'Fall on us'; and to the hills, 'Cover us.'"

## THERE THEY CRUCIFIED HIM

*Matthew 27:33–44; Mark 15:22–32;*
*Luke 23:32–38; John 19:17–24*

WHEN they had passed outside the city wall, they came to a place called Golgotha, which means "The place of a skull." The soldiers offered Jesus vinegar mingled with gall to drink, to deaden His sensibilities. a bitter liquid But when Jesus tasted it, He would not drink it. And they crucified Him, and sat down to watch over Him there. It was the third hour, or nine o'clock in the morning, when they crucified Him. Then two thieves were crucified with Him, one on the right hand and one on the left.

Then the uplifted Saviour, speaking His

69

first Word from the Cross, prayed, "Father, forgive them; for they know not what they do."

When the soldiers had crucified Jesus they took His garments and divided them into four parts, one part for each soldier. But His undergarment was without a seam, woven throughout. So the soldiers said to one another, "Let us not tear it, but let us cast lots for it to see whose it shall be." This they did, says John, in fulfillment of the Scripture, "They divided my clothing among them, and for my garments they cast lots."

a way of finding out who gets first choice

As an intended insult to the Jews, Pilate wrote a title and put it on the cross. The title read, "JESUS OF NAZARETH, THE KING OF THE JEWS." Many of the Jews read this title, for the place where Jesus was crucified was near the city of Jerusalem; and it was written in Hebrew, and in Greek, and in Latin. The chief priests of the Jews did not like this, and objected to Pilate, saying, "Do not write 'The King of the Jews'; but that he said, 'I am King of the Jews.' " But Pilate refused their request, retorting, "What I have written I have written."

The people who stood watching and who passed by the scene of the crucifixion derided Jesus on His cross, wagging their heads and saying, "You who would destroy the temple and build it in three days, save yourself. If you are the Son of God, come down from the cross." And in like manner, the chief priests, with the scribes and elders, mocked Him, say-

made fun of

71

*Two thieves were crucified with Jesus, one on the right hand and one on the left* ing, "He saved others; he cannot save himself. If he is the King of Israel, let him now come down from the cross, and we will believe him. He trusted in God; let Him deliver him now, if He will have him; for he said, 'I am the Son of God.'" And even the thieves who were crucified with Him hurled the same insults.

## THE PENITENT THIEF

*Luke 23:39–43*

kept talking and
shouting in an
angry way

LUKE alone gives the detailed story of the conduct of the two criminals who were crucified with Jesus. One of them <u>railed</u> at Jesus on the central cross, saying, "If you are the Christ, save yourself and us." But the other thief rebuked him, saying, "Do you not fear God, seeing that you are under the same condemnation of death? And we indeed justly, for we are being given the due reward for our deeds; but this man has done nothing amiss." And then in a prayer of penitence and faith he said to the Saviour, "Jesus, Lord, remember me when you come into your kingdom." And the forgiving Saviour, hearing his prayer for pardon and mercy, replied, in His second Word from the Cross, "Truly I say to you, to-

heaven

day you shall be with me in <u>paradise</u>."

## HIS FRIENDS AT THE CROSS

*John 19:25–27*

belonging to a
person who is sorry
for wrongdoing

SHORTLY after the <u>penitent's</u> prayer for pardon, there drew near the cross of Jesus five of His faithful friends. One of them was John, the beloved disciple, and the other four were women. Two of these were members of Jesus' family, namely, His own mother and His mother's sister Salome. The other two women were Mary the wife of Cleophas, and Mary Magdalene. The suffering Saviour was greatly comforted by their presence.

When Jesus saw His mother and John standing by His cross, He addressed to them His third Word from the Cross. To His mother He said, "Woman, behold your son." By this He meant that He was giving John to her as a son to take His place. To his beloved disciple, Jesus said, "Behold your mother." By this He meant that He was committing His mother to John's care. And from that hour the disciple took her to his own home.

## THE DARKNESS OVER CALVARY

*Matthew 27:45–49; Mark 15:33–36;*
*Luke 23:44–45*

Now from the sixth hour, or noon, until the ninth hour, or three o'clock in the afternoon, there was darkness over all the earth. And about the ninth hour Jesus uttered His fourth Word. from the Cross, crying out with a loud voice, in His own native Aramaic tongue, *"Eli, Eli, lama sabachthani?"* that is, "My God, my God, why hast thou forsaken me?" This awful cry of loneliness and suffering was misunderstood by those who were near the cross. Some of those standing by, when they heard it, said, "This man is calling for Elijah." And one of the soldiers, feeling sympathy for the Master, ran and took a sponge, filled it with vinegar, put it on a reed, and gave it to Him to drink. But the rest of the crowd said, "Let us wait and see whether Elijah will come to save him."

## THE SAVIOUR'S THIRST

*John 19:28–30*

JOHN relates that after this Jesus, knowing that all had now been accomplished in fulfillment of the Scripture, uttered His fifth Word from the Cross, saying, "I thirst." The soldiers had a vessel full of vinegar standing near; so they filled a sponge with the vinegar, a large growing bush put it on a plant called hyssop, and held it to sometimes used in His mouth. When Jesus had received the vine-Jewish ceremonies. gar, He uttered His sixth Word from the Cross, saying, "It is finished."

## THE DEATH OF JESUS

*Matthew 27:50; Mark 15:37;*
*Luke 23:46; John 19:30*

WHILE the four Evangelists describe the death of Jesus, Luke is the only one who records the seventh and final Word from the Cross spoken by the Saviour before He died.

According to Luke, Jesus cried out loudly, saying, "Father, into your hands I commend my spirit." And having spoken this prayer of trust to His heavenly Father, Jesus bowed His head and gave up the ghost.

put in someone's keeping

## THE ACCOMPANYING EVENTS

*Matthew 27:51–56; Mark 15:38–41;*
*Luke 23:47–49*

THE death of Jesus on the cross was accompanied by certain strange and terrifying events. In the city of Jerusalem, the great veil hanging in the sanctuary of the temple was torn in two, from top to bottom, by some mysterious power. And there was a great earthquake, and the rocks were split asunder. The graves were opened, and many bodies of the saints that had been asleep arose and came out of the graves after Christ's resurrection and went into the holy city and appeared to many. At the cross, when the centurion and those who were with him keeping watch over Jesus saw the earthquake and all the things that happened, they were greatly afraid, and said of Jesus, "Truly this was the Son of God."

into pieces

And all the people who had come together at Calvary to see the sight, when they saw all the things that had happened, beat their breasts in terror and remorse and returned home.

75

There were also many loyal and faithful women present, looking on from afar, who had followed Jesus from Galilee and who had ministered to His needs. Among these good women were Mary Magdalene, and Mary the mother of James and Joseph, and the mother of James and John, the sons of Zebedee.

## JESUS' DEATH CERTIFIED

*John 19:31–37*

JOHN says that because it was the day of preparation for the Passover, in order that the bodies might not remain on the cross on the sabbath day (for that sabbath was a high day), the Jews asked Pilate to break their legs to hasten death, so that they might be taken away.

So the soldiers came and with their heavy mallets broke the legs of the two thieves who had been crucified with Him. But when they came to Jesus and saw that He was already dead, they did not break His legs. But one of the soldiers pierced His side with a sharp spear, and instantly there came out blood and water.

says for sure John <u>affirms</u> that he was an eyewitness of these things, and that he is giving a true report in order that others might believe. He also states that these things were done in fulfillment of two prophecies from the Scriptures. One of these was: "A bone of him shall not be broken." And the other was: "They shall look on him whom they pierced."

# The Burial of Jesus

*Matthew 27:57–66; Mark 15:42–47; Luke 23:50–56; John 19:38–42*

THE Apostles' Creed says of Jesus, "He was crucified, dead, and buried." After the enemies of Jesus had put Him to death on the cross, the dead Saviour came once more into the hands of His friends. So it was that Good Friday, the darkest day in the world, came to a close with a bright and tranquil twilight hour. Three hours remained of the day on which Jesus died. The sabbath began at six o'clock in the evening.

calm and peaceful

As evening drew rapidly on, a kind man by the name of Joseph, from the Jewish town of Arimathea, came forward to render a beautiful service to the dead Saviour. Joseph was an honored member of the sanhedrin, or council; a good and righteous man, who had not consented to the decision and deed of the council in condemning Jesus to death. He was also himself seeking the kingdom of God, and was a disciple of Jesus, but secretly, for fear of the Jews. But now Joseph had the courage to go to Pilate and ask for the body of Jesus. Pilate wondered if Jesus were already dead; and calling the centurion to him he asked him whether Jesus had died. When the centurion told him that Jesus was dead, he agreed to give the body to Joseph.

Another secret disciple, Nicodemus, who had at first come to Jesus by night, also came and brought a mixture of <u>myrrh and aloes,</u> about a hundred pounds <u>weight.</u> These two generous men, assisted by other kind friends, took the body of Jesus down from the cross, and wrapped it in clean linen clothes with the spices, as was the burial custom of the Jews.

oils and drugs used in burial

Now near the place where Jesus was crucified there was a garden, and in this garden Joseph of Arimathea had prepared his own new grave, which he had <u>hewn</u> in the rock, and in which no one had ever yet been laid. Thus, because it was the Jews' day of preparation for the Passover, and as the grave was close at hand, they laid Jesus there. They rolled a great stone to the entrance of the tomb, and went away. The women who had come with Jesus from Galilee followed, and saw the tomb, and how His body was laid to rest. Among these faithful women were Mary Magdalene, and Mary the mother of James and Joseph. The women returned to their homes, and prepared spices and ointments. On the sabbath day they rested according to the commandment.

carved out

The next day, following the day of preparation, the chief priests and the Pharisees came together before Pilate and said, "Sir, we remember that that deceiver said, while he was still alive, 'After three days I will rise again.' Command therefore that the tomb be made secure until the third day, lest his disciples go by night and steal him away, and say to the people, 'He has risen from the dead,' so that the last deception will be worse than the first." Pilate granted their request, saying, "You may have your soldiers keep watch; go, make it as secure as you can." So they went and made the tomb secure by sealing the stone and by setting a watch.